Businesse[...] On Each Other

Printed in Mexico

ISBN-13: 978-0-15-352767-8
ISBN-10: 0-15-352767-6

2 3 4 5 6 7 8 9 10   050   11 10 09 08 07 06

Harcourt

SCHOOL PUBLISHERS

Visit *The Learning Site!* www.harcourtschool.com

Betsy's Bakery

Betsy's Bakery is a business. It makes bread and cakes. People buy these goods. The bakery also sells its goods to other stores.

The Sandwich Shop

The Sandwich Shop buys Betsy's bread. This shop makes good sandwiches. Sometimes the Sandwich Shop trades sandwiches with Betsy's Bakery. The bakery gives them cakes.

Harry's Auto Place

Betsy's Bakery uses trucks to carry goods. Sometimes their trucks break down. Broken trucks go to Harry's Auto Place. Betsy's Bakery needs Harry's Auto Place to fix their trucks.

The auto workers like the Sandwich Shop. It's right next door. The workers get the sandwiches they like best.

The Bank

The owners of Betsy's Bakery put their money into Hamilton Bank. The owners of other businesses do, too. The bank keeps their money safe.

Business owners borrow money from Hamilton Bank. They make improvements to their businesses. Businesses and banks need each other to get their jobs done.

Think and Respond

1. What goods does Betsy's Bakery make?

2. What service does Harry's Auto Place provide?

3. Which businesses depend on the Sandwich Shop?

4. Why do many of the business owners put their money into Hamilton Bank?

Activity

Think of a product or service that your community needs. Come up with a plan for a business. Decide how the business will help the community.